They Fought for Freedom

Steve Biko

Linda Price

Series Editor: John Pampallis

Consulting Editor: Chris van Wyk

Maskew Miller
Longman

Maskew Miller Longman (Pty) Ltd
Howard Drive, Pinelands, Cape Town

Offices in Johannesburg, Durban, Port Elizabeth, Kimberley,
King William's Town, Pietersburg, Nelspruit, Umtata and Mafikeng,
and representatives throughout southern Africa.

© Maskew Miller Longman (Pty) Ltd 1992

All rights reserved. No part of this publication may be reproduced,
stored in a retrieval system, or transmitted in any form or by
any means, electronic, mechanical, photocopying, recording,
or otherwise, without the prior written permission of the copyright holder.

First published 1992

ISBN 0 636 01660 9

Book and cover design by Nina Jawitz
Illustrations by Trish de Villiers
Typeset by Beverley Visser
Imagesetting by Castle Graphics
Printed by CTP Book Printers

Acknowledgements

The authors and publishers would like to thank the following institutions or
organisations for the use of artwork:

The *Daily Dispatch* for the cover photograph.

In some cases the publishers have been unable to get in touch with copyright holders
but they will be happy to make appropriate arrangements at the first opportunity.

Other books in the series:	Titles in preparation:
Seretse Khama	Abdul Abdurahman
Sol Plaatje	James Calata
Z.K. Matthews	Yusuf Dadoo
	John Dube
	Ruth First
	Bram Fisher
	Albert Luthuli
	Lillian Ngoyi
	Dorothy Zihlangu

Contents

Before We Begin Our Story		iv
Chapter 1:	Early Years	1
Chapter 2:	Education and Beginnings of Political Involvement	4
Chapter 3:	What is Black Consciousness?	12
Chapter 4:	Banning and Continued Political Activities	19
Chapter 5:	The Soweto Uprising	23
Chapter 6:	Biko's Final Arrest and Detention	30
Chapter 7:	People's Anger and Government Lies	35
Chapter 8:	The Funeral	39
Chapter 9:	The Inquest	41
Chapter 10:	Conclusion	46
Learn these Words and Phrases		48
Activities		50
More Books about Biko		57

Before We Begin Our Story

At the entrance to Ginsberg township, near King William's Town in the Eastern Cape, lies a small cemetery. Here the marble headstone of one of South Africa's leaders stands firmly in the ground.

> BANTU STEPHEN BIKO
> Honorary President
> BLACK PEOPLE'S CONVENTION
> born 18 – 12 – 1946
> died 12 – 9 – 1977
> ONE AZANIA ONE NATION

Steve Biko died at the young age of thirty, but he is remembered as one of the great leaders of the black people in their fight against apartheid in South Africa. The ideas of Black Consciousness which he worked hard to reinforce amongst the black people had their roots in organisations which the government had banned in 1960, namely the African National Congress (ANC) and the Pan African Congress (PAC). These organisations expressed the hopes and needs of the black people who were denied basic rights like the right to vote for the government, equal education and the right to choose where they want to live.

In March 1960, the police opened fire and killed 69 black people who were demonstrating against the pass laws at Sharpeville. Then the government tried to destroy black opposition to apartheid by banning the ANC and the PAC. It imprisoned some of their leaders while others managed to flee the country. During the next few years black opposition to apartheid in South Africa was virtually destroyed. Black people were left with no organisations through which to channel their problems and to express their anger against apartheid. Steve Biko and other Black Consciousness leaders realised the need to continue the work of the older liberation movements and, in the late 1960s, they formed the South African Students Organisation (SASO) and the Black Peoples' Convention (BPC).

This book tells the story of Steve Biko and the Black Consciousness Movement that he strove so hard to build amongst the black people in South Africa.

> We are looking forward to a non-racial, just and equal society in which colour, religion and race shall form no point of reference.
>
> **(Steve Biko**, 1972)

Map with details of Steve Biko's life

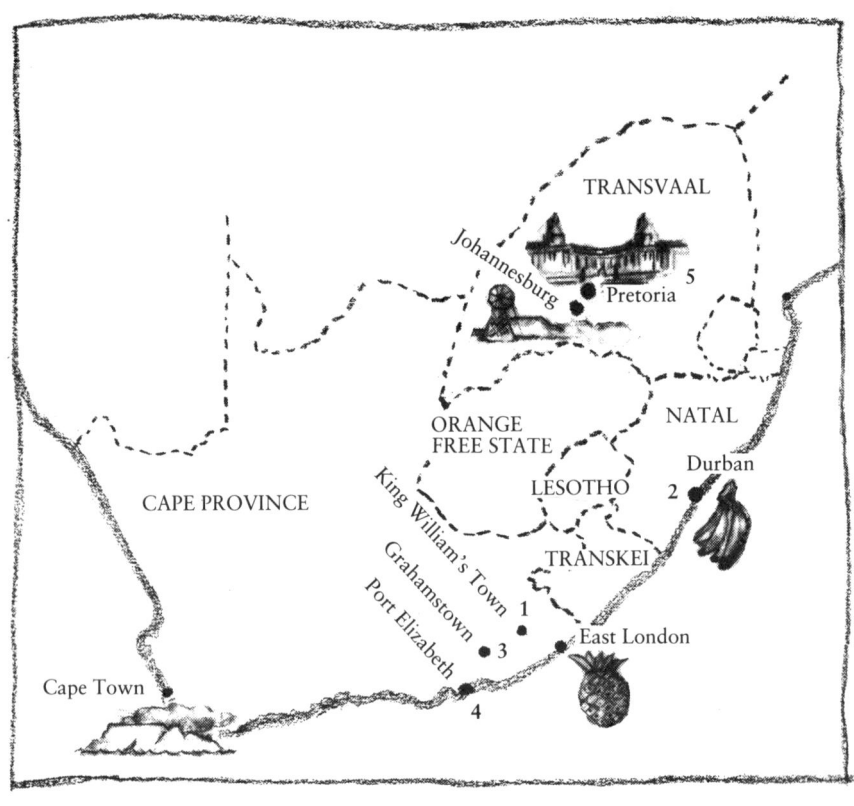

1. Born in King William's Town, 1946
2. Studied at the University of Natal Medical School, 1966–1972
3. Arrested near Grahamstown, 1977
4. Detained by police in Port Elizabeth
5. Died in the Pretoria prison, 12 September 1977

1

Early Years

The red African sunset silhouetted the figure of a young boy as he walked briskly along the dust path. The path weaved through the open veld, scattered with patches of grass, rocks and cactus plants. As the red and orange sky deepened in colour, the distant rolling hills darkened and the yellow veld shimmered.

The path merged with a wide dust-road which was lined with telegraph wires on either side. The wires stretched in loops above the ground and were joined at intervals by long, thin poles which stood upright on the ground. The shrill sounds of the birds perched daintily on the thin wires beckoned the twilight hour.

It was Sunday evening. The young boy had spent the afternoon reading in the cool shade of a wattle tree. He loved to read and you would often see him heading for the open veld with a book or two tucked firmly under his arm.

The sun was fast fading. But the intense heat still dragged through the air. The boy's bare feet sank into the warm sand sending up little clouds of dust. His eyes shone and the trail of his footprints remained in the sand behind his moving figure as he made his way home. It is the journey marked by these footprints that we shall follow to learn about the life of Bantu Stephen Biko.

Steve's long legs hastened into a rapid stride. Dinner time was fast approaching and he should wash and get ready for the evening meal.

The weekends were special as the family could spend more time together than during the week. When Steve was only four years old, his father, Mzimgayi, died. Since this time, Steve's older brother had played the role of head of the family. Steve also had an older and a younger sister. Steve's father had worked as a clerk and his mother was a domestic worker for white families in and around King William's Town. The Biko family was christian and Sundays had a special importance to them as a holy day.

Before long Steve reached the outskirts of Ginsberg township where he lived. In the distance he saw the columns of smoke rising above the flat zinc roofs of the houses. He passed a group of lively children at the side of the road. They smiled cheekily at him. They had spent the day selling carved wooden animals to passing motorists. As another car zoomed past they waved their giraffe and buck in the dust that it left behind.

Steve passed a large aluminium water reservoir at the entrance to the township. In a few minutes Steve would be at the front gate of his house. He stopped briefly to greet Mr Nkomo, the caretaker of the local church. The old man sat on a rock alongside the road. He puffed heavily on his long wooden pipe and leaned forward on his battered cane. His dog dozed quietly at his feet. Mr Nkomo's wrinkled face creased into a smile.

2

"Hello, young Steve," he shouted, "been out in the veld with your books again?"

Steve laughed and bent down to pat the dog's head. The dog nudged his moist warm nose into the palm of Steve's hand and thumped his tail affectionately.

At that moment a young white couple drove by. Their large red car sent the dust whirling about in the air. It was seldom that white people ever visited the township and the car had a King William's Town number-plate. Mr Nkomo rose to his feet and Steve could hear the click-click of his joints as he stood up. Mr Nkomo raised his torn black hat, bowed his grey head, and called: "*Goeienaand Baas, goeienaand* Madam" ("Good evening Boss, good evening Madam"). His croaky voice was absorbed by the exhaust fumes as the car sped down the road.

Steve looked at the old man and frowned. Then suddenly he remembered the pot on the stove at home. It would probably be filling the house with its mouthwatering aroma of meat and potatoes. He said goodbye to Mr Nkomo and his dog.

As he scuttled home Steve wondered about the white couple who had driven by a moment ago. They looked far younger than the old man, yet he had struggled to his feet to greet them. "Is it not the wise Mr Nkomo who deserves a show of respect?" Steve thought. People constantly turned to him for practical advice, and he also knew of all kinds of remedies for illnesses.

The smell of freshly baked bread filtered through the air towards Steve, and he could hear his mother and sisters in the kitchen. He hummed softly as he opened the front door.

Other Ginsberg township dwellers were also settling down for the evening. The orange glow of the gas lamps reflected in the windows of the rows of houses, and the zinc roofs shone in the evening glare. A barefoot boy pushed a wire truck along one of the empty streets, and an elderly husband and wife sat in their chairs outside the front door of their house. The couple looked out over the quiet streets. The people of Ginsberg were preparing for another week at work and at school.

Education and Beginnings of Political Involvement

Steve's sharp mind and eagerness to learn made him a very bright scholar. He attended primary and secondary schools in King William's Town and later moved to Natal. There he completed his school education at St Francis College, a Roman Catholic school in Marianhill, near Pinetown.

When Steve was 17 years old his older brother was jailed for his political activities. It was 1963 and the police arrested hundreds of young political activists across South Africa. It was very possibly the arrest of Steve's brother that sparked off his interest in politics.

He matriculated at the end of 1965, and had done so well that he won a scholarship to study at the University of Natal Medical School. At the time this was the only school where black people could study medicine.

The following year Steve began his medical training, and if work came easily to him, so did play. Steve enjoyed sport and he played lock-forward for the university rugby team. But medicine and sport were not Steve's only priorities in life.

He was deeply concerned about the unfair and harsh treatment of black people under apartheid in South Africa. While he was studying in Natal he became actively involved in politics. Soon after enrolling at university, Steve was voted on to the Students Representative Council (SRC). Through the SRC he became involved with the National Union of South African Students (NUSAS).

NUSAS had a long history of opposition to apartheid, and was so outspoken that in 1963 the Minster of Justice, John Vorster had called this student organisation "a cancer in the life of the nation". During the 1960s the white nationalist government arrested, banned and imprisoned many people who were involved in politics.

In the late 1960s the students played a big part in campaigning against the injustices in South Africa, and Steve was a leader amongst these students. He was respected and admired by his fellow students for his warm nature and strong leadership abilities. Students who worked with Steve at the University of Natal described how he never dominated activities and often spoke very little during political discussions. At the end of the day, however, they would always look to him for guidance.

NUSAS was made up mainly of white students of the liberal Universities of Cape Town, Witwatersrand, Natal and Rhodes. NUSAS was banned at the newly-formed bantustan universities as well as at the Universities of Durban-Westville (for Indians) and the Western Cape (for coloureds). The laws of the land and the lack of educational opportunities for black people meant that there were very few black students anywhere in the country. It is not surprising then, that a student organisation such as NUSAS would be dominated by whites.

This domination increased after 1959 when the government passed the Extension of Universities Act. This act allowed only limited numbers of black students to enrol at "white" universities such as the Universities of Cape Town, Witwatersrand and Natal where NUSAS operated.

Steve and other black students felt that their fellow white students in NUSAS did not have an understanding of the experiences of black people. The life-styles of blacks and whites were very different. Although the white students were also against apartheid, they had grown up and lived in the white suburbs and had attended white schools. These schools offered much better facilities (classrooms, quality of teachers, libraries) and a better education than black schools.

A central obstacle faced by whites and blacks in NUSAS was obviously the legal restrictions of apartheid. The law ensured that the number of white students far outweighed those of black students at universities. In Grahamstown, during the

NUSAS conference in 1967, the blacks had to stay at a church building while the whites stayed in residence around the conference site. Their living conditions in the church building were appalling and they had to be transported to the conference site in cars each day. Events like this made blacks feel inferior to whites.

One evening after a rugby practice Steve and his friends were relaxing on the stands. As usual they talked politics. And soon they started to discuss the possibility of forming a separate organisation for black students.

"This is not the first time we've discussed the idea of a black student organisation," Steve said. "We have all been thinking about it quite a lot."

"We have, we have," the others nodded.

"I've just come back from visiting my cousin at the Indians-only University of Durban-Westville," Ben Mzimela said.

"The students there are not even allowed to participate openly in NUSAS."

"Why?" Ben asked, and got up to answer his own question.

"Because NUSAS is banned at the universities where most black students study."

"Well, it's not surprising then," said Peter Shongwe, "that NUSAS is dominated by whites. And for some reason we seem to accept this. It's the same with the Christian group I work with. All of us – black and white – seem to accept that the leaders should be white."

Steve said that all student groups were mainly concerned with problems affecting white students. Black concerns were not given equal attention. On the other hand, an organisation which had only black membership would be able to concentrate on black problems. But he also added that it was not advisable to divide the student population into separate groups on the basis of colour. This, he said, would appear to be in support of apartheid.

Ben nodded in agreement. He said that organisations based on colour tend to build up resentment and to widen the gap between the different races of South Africa. And this was indeed something which the student community had fought hard against.

There was a long silence. The decision as to whether the black students should break away from NUSAS and form their own organisation was not an easy one. It still required much thought and debate.

The sun had already set and the friends started to head for home.

"As a matter of principle we must reject separation," Steve said as they walked across the playing fields. "This would certainly be the case in a normal society."

"But," he went on, "South Africa is not a normal society and it is difficult not to see whites as a group of people who want to maintain apartheid."

Most black students were not hostile towards their white fellow students. However, they recognised that black people had different needs to those of whites. NUSAS, they felt, was not able to serve the needs of black students properly.

In December 1968, after much debate, the black students led by Steve, formed their own organisation. They called it the South African Students Organisation (SASO).

SASO, like NUSAS, had branches on a number of university campuses, and Steve was elected president of the new organisation.

This was the first step on Biko's journey to persuade black people that they should be proud to be black and demand that their rights be respected. Along with other leaders of SASO like Barney Pityana and Abram Tiro, Steve travelled around the country visiting the black universities and speaking to fellow students.

SASO recognised that it was important to build close links with the black community. They were privileged to attend university, but they knew this did not give them the right to lead the fight against apartheid. They wanted to express the needs and grievances of black people. And in order to do this successfully, they had to be in touch with the feelings of black people as a whole.

The students held meetings with people from various communities, and worked on community projects.

Over the years SASO made headway in carrying out its objectives. But sometimes it did make mistakes. One of these mistakes happened in a shanty town called Newfarm in Inanda near Durban.

In the early 1970s many of the Newfarm shacks were destroyed in a big flood.

"We must help these people," said Steve to some of his comrades. "They are too poor to buy the materials to rebuild their homes."

"But we're student activists interested in politics," one young student said. "Why do we have to help rebuild shacks?"

"We need to work side by side with the people," Steve explained. "In this way we can get to know them well and also discuss our political ideas with them."

Steve's comrades agreed with him. And a few days later a group of students – all SASO members – went into Newfarm carrying corrugated iron sheets, tools, and other equipment.

"We have come to help you to fix up your homes," they told the Newfarm residents.

The people agreed to let them help, and even showed them how to build. But they did not join in the work; they just watched and gave advice.

The students dug holes for wooden poles. They nailed sheets of zinc together. They sawed, carried, cut their fingers, and

sweated in the humid Natal heat. And the residents relaxed underneath a tree.

The students grew more and more annoyed with their "advisers" in the shade. Eventually they decided to confront these ungrateful people.

"We're trying to help you to rebuild your homes," said the students, trying to be as polite as possible. "Why don't you people help?"

"Why should we?" came the reply. "We are not being paid. At least the government is paying you to do this work."

Suddenly it all made sense to the shocked, but also amused, students. The people thought that they had been sent by the government to help them. The SASO activists realised that they should have discussed the whole matter with the community first. If they had done this they would not have been misunderstood. SASO had learned an important political lesson.

They then explained to the people who they were and what they were trying to do. And eventually everyone joined in the work.

Although Steve led a very busy life with his political activities and his studies, he also found time for romance. Nontsikelela Mashalaba, called Ntsiki for short, lived in Umtata, the capital city of the Transkei. She was training to become a nurse when she met and fell in love with Steve.

Steven and Ntsiki were married in 1970, and later had two sons. They named their elder son Nkosinathi which means "the Lord is with us". Samora, their second son, was named after the president of Mozambique, Samora Machel.

Steve admired Machel because he was leading the people of Mozambique in their fight for independence from colonial rule. Steve read continually about the war between Frelimo (Front for the Liberation of Mozambique) and the Portuguese government. And Steve's own political work was inspired by the determination and strength of Machel and his people.

Unfortunately Steve did not have enough time for his studies because of his political work. In 1972, at the end of his third year, he was expelled from the university. The administration said it was because of poor academic performance. Steve never completed his medical degree, deciding instead to devote his life to working against injustice in South Africa.

There were people who did not like the political work which Steve was doing. The security police watched him and harassed him whenever they could. They frequently followed him around town and woke him up in the middle of the night to search his home.

Despite this bullying by the government, Steve's political commitment grew stronger. He had put all his political energy into the work of SASO but he did not think that university people should be the only voice of the black people. So in 1972 he and other SASO leaders called a meeting of black organisations from all over South Africa.

Trade unionists, students, and church and community groups came together, and a new organisation called the Black People's Convention (BPC) was formed.

Both SASO and the BPC believed in the ideas of Black Consciousness. But what is Black Consciousness? And why was it important for black people in their struggle for freedom? The following chapter will examine Black Consciousness, as expressed by Steve Biko and his followers.

What is Black Consciousness?

Although there were many gifted leaders of the Black Consciousness Movement, it was the name of Steve Biko that stood out amongst this large group. Steve was, however, a modest man and he did not think of himself as the head of the movement. He encouraged all the leaders to work as a group, and to share their tasks and responsibilities.

The movement aimed to unite and strengthen black people and to overcome feelings of inferiority. Black Consciousness encouraged feelings of pride amongst all those who were discriminated against on the grounds of colour or race, and therefore united all the oppressed people: coloured, Indian and African. It rejected the word "non-white" which was used by the government, and instead used the word "black".

This was because "non-white" was a negative term. It described people in terms of what they were not, instead of what they were. As such, it conveyed the racist impression that there was something inferior or wrong in being black.

When the white nationalist government came to power in 1948, the cruel apartheid laws that it introduced treated black people as inferior to white people. Blacks and whites were forced to live in separate areas, attend

separate schools, and make use of separate amenities such as cinemas and restaurants.

Blacks were not allowed to vote and they had to carry special documents of identity (pass books) with them wherever they went. They were prevented from doing certain categories of work and marriages between blacks and whites were forbidden. The places where whites lived, worked and played were always far better than those reserved for blacks.

All these laws, together with the power of the government's army and police force, made many black people feel that they were powerless. Some even felt that they were not as good or as clever as whites. After the government banned the ANC and the PAC in 1960, and put a large number of their leaders in prison, many people felt that there was nothing they could do to end their oppression.

Steve and his comrades did not agree. They said that blacks had to become proud of their blackness and throw off any ideas that they were not as good as whites. Only if they did this would they be able to struggle to free themselves. The words of Heaku Rachidi, a Black Consciousness activist, sum up the feeling of the time:

> "We are not aberrations of white people but are black people in our own right."

The Black Consciousness Movement started up a few community projects such as clinics and community centres, and was strongly committed to self-help schemes. This movement believed that blacks could no longer be led and dominated by whites. The self-help clinics and community centres started by the movement raised their own money and trained their own staff. Crafts and trades were taught at these community centres, and once people had been trained they could go out into the community and earn their living. These organisations helped people to feel a sense of pride in their ability to live meaningful lives and they did not feel totally dependent on the government for their well-being.

Black Consciousness was also expressed through cultural

activities like poetry and drama. It was a positive cultural energy; a proud and defiant expression of being black. T-shirts bearing the clenched fist (the symbol of black unity) and slogans like "Black is Beautiful" were printed, and poems like the following were written:

> "*I*
> *am the liberator*
> *no*
> *white man can liberate me*
> *only*
> *a black man can free himself.*"
>
> *Anonymous*

In many ways this cultural expression resembled that of Martin Luther King's civil rights campaign in the United States of America during the 1960s.

Steve soon became a popular spokesperson for Black Consciousness. One afternoon he spoke at a meeting held by the BPC in a church hall in Durban. Black people – workers, students, teachers, the unemployed – surged into the hall to listen to the voice of Black Consciousness.

Banners hung on the walls boldly shouting out the pride of being black, and the importance of fighting for freedom, with slogans like "South Africa belongs to Us" or "We remember our Leaders" and "The People shall Govern!" Some people even wore the colours – yellow, black and green – of the banned ANC. Microphones crackled with the voices of leaders calling for unity, declaring war against apartheid.

The aged had almost forgotten the brave leaders who sat in prison, or were in exile. The young had never heard these leaders – or set eyes on them. But the Black Consciousness Movement was bridging the political vacuum that had existed in South Africa since the government tried to suppress all opposition to apartheid in the 1960s.

A wonderful sense of pride filled the hall that day. The struggle had begun again. Steve Biko – one of their leaders – was about to speak.

The crowd welcomed Steve and other Black Consciousness speakers with songs and applause. In between the speeches the building echoed with cheers and shouts of "*Amandla ... Amandla ... Ngawethu!*" (Power to the people). The local pastor sat with Steve and his friends behind a long table. A large banner draped across the front of the table declared "Black People's Convention" in huge bold letters.

Steve was the final speaker that afternoon. He rounded off the meeting by emphasising the unity of black people.

"We are oppressed, not as individuals, not as Zulus, Xhosas, Vendas, or Indians. We are oppressed because we are black. We must unite ourselves and respond as a strong force."

15

At that point a young man called Vusi stood up and shouted excitedly, "*Ja*, one day we'll be driving around in the BMWs and Mercs!"

The audience burst into loud laughter and everyone cheered. Steve smiled broadly and gently shook his head.

He waited for the laughter to die down and then he said, "Brothers and sisters, we must think carefully about what we are saying and feeling here ..."

The people quietened down and Steve continued in his calm, steady voice.

> "It is true that the majority of the South African population is black, and yet all the political and economic power is in the hands of the white minority. Whites are protected by the laws from competition with blacks in employment, sport and politics, and they have higher standards of living, education and salaries. This is part and parcel of government policy of keeping the different racial groups separate from one another. The obvious and sad outcome is that blacks and whites have developed suspicions about one another.
>
> "It is not, however, our task to reinforce this. The Black Consciousness Movement is not anti-white. It is important that we all understand this, both blacks and whites. We must all look, and work actively, towards a future South Africa that is free from racial hatred.
>
> "This means that we, the black people of South Africa, must work towards becoming self-sufficient, politically, socially and economically. In this way we will gain confidence and pride. But this is not to say that we must become anti-white. The issue is not whether blacks or whites are wealthy enough to drive BMWs, but that we all share in the wealth of the land."

The audience listened carefully to what Steve said. When he sat down they chatted quietly amongst themselves. Although it was difficult not to feel anger and hatred towards white people, most agreed that these feelings would not help to change South Africa into a free and non-racial country. Indeed, the whole idea behind this change was to build a future South Africa in which all its people would live together in a fair and democratic society.

Many South Africans did not agree with Steve's ideas. Among these were liberal whites who felt that Black Consciousness was racist and anti-white. These liberals believed that the only way in which apartheid could be opposed was through integration between blacks and whites.

One such person was Donald Woods who was the editor of the *Daily Dispatch* in East London. Woods frequently criticised the ideas of Steve and the Black Consciousness Movement in his newspaper.

It was only later when Steve and Donald became firm friends that Donald began to understand and accept Black Consciousness.

In the many discussions Steve and Donald had together, Steve explained why he believed it was important for black organisations to move away from white liberals. He argued that this was because blacks had grown dependent on whites, and for years the white liberal had been the spokesperson of black demands. These paternalistic attitudes of liberals undermined black people's independence and belief in themselves.

Some black activists also believed that whites and blacks should unite and work together to fight apartheid. But Steve and his followers felt that black people must first shed the feelings of inferiority that apartheid had caused. Only then could blacks and whites work together as equals to oppose the racist system of government. It was common practice in multiracial organisations for whites to tell blacks how to fight oppression. Steve felt that this was no longer acceptable, however good their intentions.

Because Steve was always a spokesperson for peace, his Black Consciousness philosophy was respected and supported by many liberal whites in South Africa and by politicians in Europe and America.

It is important, however, to understand that change could never come about peacefully in South Africa under apartheid. This is because apartheid itself was violent. This will become very clear as we trace the events of Steve's life.

Banning and Continued Political Activities

After Steve left medical school in June 1972, he remained in Durban and worked full-time for the Black Community Programmes which he had helped to build. He knew the needs of the black community and he believed in self-help.

The apartheid laws and inferior Bantu education and medical services made it very difficult for black people to learn skills and to have the medical care that they needed. Black Community Programmes taught people how to read and write, and skills such as weaving and dress-making. Health education was also an important part of the programmes.

But soon Steve was forced to leave Durban. He worked on a political journal called *Black Review 1972* which the government banned in February 1973. Later, Steve himself, along with other members of SASO and BPC, was also banned by the government. This meant that he was no longer allowed to do any political work. He was also forced to return to King William's Town, the small town in the Eastern Cape where he was born. Because Steve was banned he was not allowed to leave the town for the next five years.

However, Steve did not want to sit around and waste five years. He therefore decided to study law by correspondence, and registered with the University of South Africa (UNISA). Steve's banning meant that he could not attend any meeting or write for newspapers, magazines or books; nor could anything that he said be quoted. He was not allowed to talk to two or more people at the same time; even his friends could only visit him one at a time.

Steve had become known overseas and he was invited by the Catholic Justice and Peace Commission to attend a conference in Germany. But the South African government refused to give him a passport.

Steve was not allowed to enter certain buildings such as courts, educational institutions and the offices of newspapers and other publishers. The Biko home was frequently visited by the police and they would search the entire house to look for evidence of any political activity.

Steve's life was full of tensions but he was still determined to continue his political work and he had to be on the alert at all times so that the security police would not catch him. This was made more difficult by the 24 hour police watch outside his house. He was arrested and detained many times but he refused to give in.

Steve continued to work for the Black Community Programmes as Executive Director for the Eastern Cape. It was his job to co-ordinate the activities of the programmes which were carried out throughout the country.

In 1975 he played a leading role in the formation of the Zimele Trust Fund and the Ginsberg Educational Trust. Appropriately, "Zimele" means "Stand on Your Own". Church and overseas organisations which were opposed to apartheid in South Africa put money into these trusts.

Black Consciousness in the 1970s saw an increase in political activity. This meant that scores of people were being imprisoned by the government. Many of these people were fathers and mothers who had families. The Zimele Trust took care of these families while their breadwinners were in prison. The Ginsberg Trust provided financial help for black students to study.

In 1975 Steve Biko was among many young black activists detained by the government. He was kept in prison for 137 days. After his release, the restrictions that were placed on him when he was banned in 1972 were increased. He was not allowed to have anything to do with the Black Community Programme. But this did not stop Steve from doing any work.

Steve's strength as a leader and his deep political commitment were well balanced by his warm and gentle nature. As a father, husband, friend, and political figure, he was much loved and respected. His political work meant that he was not able to spend as much time with his family as he would have liked. But Ntsiki was a strong and supportive wife and mother.

Steve loved music, especially the strong, harmonious beat of African "gumba" music. He enjoyed dancing, and he would be at the centre of the dance floor at parties. When he was "swinging" he usually dressed in a sleeveless open-necked shirt, jeans with a broad belt, and a pair of yellowish shoes.

Steve's sense of humour made many friends chuckle. Donald Woods remembers how much he enjoyed Steve's cheerful telephone calls at the office. If Steve liked Donald's editorial columns, he would call and say:

"Hiiii! Hey, man, that was a good editorial this morning! *Kwewuku! Ubabethile!*" ('Gee! You really hit them!')

It was too dangerous to convey political messages over the telephone, so if Steve wanted to inform Donald of a forthcoming meeting or an important political event that had taken place, he would send a message via a close friend called Malusa Mpumlwana.

Mpumlwana is the diminutive of *umpumlo* which means "nose". Steve would phone Donald and say:

"I'm sending a message by a small-nosed courier who should be with you in five minutes."

One of Steve's closest friends was Dr Mamphela Ramphele. Steve had first met Mamphela when they studied together at medical school.

Steve and Mamphela had first come up with the idea for the health clinics when they were students. The Zanempilo clinic was one of the main health projects of the Black Community Programmes.

The clinic was built on a hill outside King William's Town in a rural district known as Zinyoka which means "Place of Snakes" in Xhosa.

Thousands of black people who were not able to get to the main hospitals in King William's Town and nearby East London, went to this community health centre. The clinic was run by a small staff under Mamphela. It had an operating theatre, a maternity ward, and classrooms for lessons in health and hygiene.

Another great friend of Steve's was Thami Zani. He was a big, strong man who was built like a boxing champion. He once held the unfortunate record in the BPC for the longest solitary confinement when he was detained for 434 days.

Peter Jones from Cape Town was Steve's constant companion. He was full of fun and his friends called him "P.G.".

Steve was also very friendly with Father Aelred Stubbs, an Anglican priest. He had been sent out to South Africa from England in 1959 and spent many long decades working actively against the hated system of apartheid.

These were Steve's closest friends, and they worked together, along with other South Africans, to bring an end to racial oppression.

5   The Soweto Uprising

Despite the attempts of the security police to stop Steve's political work, he continued to play a leading role in the Black Consciousness Movement. In 1976 he became Secretary-General of the Zimele Trust Fund and he was also elected Honorary President of the BPC.

As Honorary President, Steve was not expected to carry out the daily tasks of a president. And it would have been impossible for him to do so as he was banned. Although he was not able to work actively amongst the people, they expressed their faith in him as their dedicated leader by voting him to this position.

Partly as a result of the hard work of Steve and his co-workers throughout the country in strengthening and uniting black people, the year 1976 was important in the history of Black Consciousness as black opposition to apartheid reached a peak.

The school students were at the centre. They refused to attend school and went out into the streets of the townships to protest against their inferior education. They were also angry because the Minister of Bantu Education had instructed that half the subjects in schools at standards five and six be taught in Afrikaans.

Many young black people were arrested. They faced charges for disruption, and for promoting the aims of Black Consciousness.

In May 1976 Steve was called as a witness in the trial of nine students who were SASO members. The students were charged with terrorism and faced the possibility of death by hanging.

The security police did not, however, have any concrete evidence to prove that these students had committed a crime. They were really being tried because they believed that apartheid was wrong and were trying to persuade others to believe in the ideas of Black Consciousness.

Although Steve was banned, the defence lawyer called him to give evidence because he was an important leader of Black Consciousness. The government tried to prove that spreading the ideas of Black Consciousness was a danger to public safety. The government said it encouraged black hatred against whites in order to overthrow the government.

The lawyer defending the students did not agree. He argued that Black Consciousness encouraged black people to seek peaceful ways to achieve their aims. It was apartheid that was to blame for hostility and mistrust between the races, and black people needed no encouragement in the anger they felt towards white racism.

Steve was the most important witness called by the defence. And this was the first time he had spoken in public for nearly three years. SASO and the BPC, the organisations which were in effect on trial, were born of Black Consciousness which Steve had helped to introduce amongst black people. In Steve's four and a half days as a defence witness, he provided the court, South Africa, and the world with the opportunity to understand the philosophy of Black Consciousness.

When asked by the defence laywer, David Soggot, to comment on Black Consciousness, Steve replied:

"Basically, Black Consciousness directs itself to the black people and their situation, and the black people are subjected to two forces in this country. They are first of all oppressed by an external world through institutionalised machinery and through laws that restrict them from doing certain things, through heavy work conditions, through poor pay, through difficult living conditions, through poor education, these are external to them.

"Secondly, and this we regard as the most important, black people in themselves have developed a certain state of alienation. They reject themselves precisely because they attach the meaning white to all that is good, in other words they equate white with good. This arises out of their living and it arises out of their development from childhood.

"When you go to school, for instance, your school is not the same as the white school, and the conclusion you reach is that the education you get there cannot be the same as what the white kids get at school.

"The black kids normally have shabby uniforms, if any, or no uniforms, while the white kids always have uniforms. You find for instance even the organisation of sport, these are things you notice as a kid, at white schools to be absolutely so thorough and indicative of good training, good upbringing.

"Now this is part of the roots of self-negation which our kids get even as they grow up. The homes are different, the streets are different, the lighting is different, so you tend to begin to feel that there is something incomplete in your humanity, and that completeness goes with whiteness. This is carried through to adulthood when black people have got to live and work."

But despite Steve's testimony, the court found the students guilty.

The anger in the townships grew. Black South Africans were inspired by the victories of liberation movements in neighbouring countries. In Mozambique Frelimo had won their fight for liberation, and South Africa's invasion of Angola a few months earlier had been defeated by Angolan and Cuban forces.

Violence erupted in Soweto, the largest black townships in South Africa, less than 20 km from Johannesburg. In the 1970s over a million people lived here in thousands of rows of bleak, tiny four-roomed houses.

On 16 June 1976, 20 000 students marched in protest in the

streets of Soweto. But the security forces opened fire on the crowd and many students were killed and injured. The black people of South Africa were shocked and angered by such cruelty and a wave of protest against the government spread throughout the country.

In the following months hundreds of people were killed and thousands were injured and imprisoned. Nevertheless, student leaders were able to organise successful boycotts of schools, close beer halls, force the Soweto Urban Bantu Council and Bantu School Boards to resign. These Bantu councils and school boards were set up by the government rather than by the people. Students also organised stay-at-home strikes and a Christmas shopping boycott.

Hector Petersen, shot by police in Soweto, 16 June 1976

By the end of October 1977, the police said that nearly 700 people had been killed, but many people claimed that the true figure was more than 1 000. In addition several thousand had been wounded.

Soweto leaders demanded that the government meet with three leaders of the black people to discuss the future of the country. These leaders were Nelson Mandela of the ANC, who was imprisoned for life on Robben Island at the time, the late Robert Sobukwe, leader of the PAC, living under banning orders in Kimberley, and Steve Biko.

The government refused to talk. But it arrested and detained many more people, and in August 1976 Steve was arrested. He was held in solitary confinement for 101 days. This meant that he was kept alone in a cell and never saw anyone apart from the prison wardens. Steve did not allow this to break his spirit and he exercised daily in his small cell and read as much as possible.

Steve's family and friends stood by him at all times. After he was released they organised a small celebration at the Zanempilo clinic. The party was held in the clinic's small lounge and Steven, Ntsiki, Mamphela and about ten other friends, including Donald Woods and his wife Wendy, drank champagne, laughed and listened to music into the early hours of the morning. Many South Africans had died and suffered but they could not stop here. The struggle would continue.

But, there were others to think of too. Just after his release Steve helped to organise a Christmas party at a crèche run by the BPC. It was a lively party and the children had a great time. The tables were filled with sweets, cakes and cold drinks, the walls and ceiling were covered with colourful pictures, and brightly wrapped presents were lying underneath a Christmas tree. It was a happy Christmas for some kids.

For many, however, it was an unhappy year. During the following months, the government continued to arrest many pupils and students, their ages ranging from 17 to 24 years. In one case 31 students were tried and sentenced to five years imprisonment each. Many other students were detained and held without trial for weeks or even months before being released.

In March 1977 Steve was again arrested, detained and later released. In July that year he was arrested yet again. This time because of his involvement in another of the many cases that arose out of the revolt of school children that began in Soweto in June 1976.

The government accused Steve of persuading seven children to say they were forced to make false statements to the police.

During his testimony in court Steve once again showed his intelligence and strength as a spokesperson and leader of the black people. He was found not guilty. The court was packed with his supporters and friends. After the magistrate had announced his verdict, the crowd cheered and shouted *Amandla*.

But it was clear that the security police were determined to make Steve suffer. He had to be extremely careful at all times.

The Soweto uprising, and the violent police response, brought about a major shift in the political climate in South Africa. It served as a bridge connecting the younger generation of black South Africans to the older generation, who had suffered the full force of the government's power in the 1950s and early 1960s.

Although the ANC was banned in South Africa, it had remained in the country as an underground movement. The government had failed to undermine the ideas and status of the ANC among the people. This meant that the youth whom the Black Consciousness Movement was organising were at least aware of the ANC, even though many had grown up without any direct contact with the ANC. The ANC had an influence among some students and its literature was circulated in the townships.

Links between the Black Consciousness Movement and the ANC had been formed in the early 1970s. But it was only after the Soweto uprising that these links extended more deeply into the black community. The ANC grew stronger both inside and outside South Africa, and thousands of young black people fled the country and joined the ANC.

Among those who joined the ANC were Black Consciousness activists. Some joined *Umkhonto we Sizwe,* the ANC's liberation army, while the ANC arranged for others to continue their studies in other countries.

The ANC had always acknowledged the importance of the Black Consciousness Movement because it worked to unite the black people of South Africa to oppose apartheid. As we mentioned earlier, these views were built on political positions that the ANC had long canvassed and fought for.

In 1976 the ANC decided that a meeting should be arranged between the leadership of the ANC and the Black Consciousness Movement. Arrangements were made in 1976 and 1977 but each time it proved impossible to bring Steve safely out of the country.

It was the Soweto uprising which made many thousands of young people join the fight against apartheid. Siphiwe, a student at the time of the Soweto uprising, later explained:

> "The thing that made me politically minded was the influence I got from 1976, because so many of our brothers and sisters were shot dead for their rights. In fact, June 16th was the day I started to have interest in political activity in this country."

Another student, Jabulani, said:

> "It was the 1976 experience that made us start to ask questions about the poverty of our people, the living conditions of our people. We started questioning why whites live that type of life and we live in these conditions, and we began to realise also that our whole education system is a very big lie. Because it's a system that tells you that certain people must be rich and others must be poor, and if people are poor, it must be their own fault. These are the values that our education system teaches us, and in 1976 we started questioning those values."

Biko's Final Arrest and Detention

On the evening of 18 August 1977, Steve was travelling home with Peter Jones from a political meeting in the Eastern Cape. Steve, as usual, had ignored his banning orders. Their car was stopped at a security police road-block near Grahamstown.

"Open the boot," one of the policemen demanded. "We want to see what you've got in there."

Steve remained seated in the car. Peter got out and went to the boot. But he had difficulty opening the boot as the lock was giving trouble. A plainclothes officer, who Steve and Peter later learned was Lieutenant Oosthuizen, asked Peter where he was going to. Peter replied that he was on his way to East London.

"*Jy gaan seker vir ou Biko sien,*" ("You're probably going to visit that chap Biko") Lieutenant Oosthuizen said.

But Peter showed no reaction and simply replied: "Who's Biko?"

Although Peter tried and tried, he still could not open the boot. The policemen were getting impatient as it was late in the night. Lieutenant Oosthuizen told Peter to follow them to the police station where the car could be searched.

The lieutenant started to walk towards his car, but then he turned around and pointed at Steve who was still seated in the car, and said to the other policemen:

"*Daai groot man kan saam met my ry, en julle ry saam met hom.*" ("That big chap can ride with me and you ride together with him.")

At the police station Peter was told to park the car under some lights. Peter and Steve were bodily searched while other policemen searched the car. Then the police asked their names. "I am Bantu Stephen Biko," Steve replied. There was a stunned silence for several moments. The police just stared at the two men.

Then they grabbed Steve and Peter and took them into the police station.

"On what grounds are you holding us here?" asked Steve.

The lieutenant just laughed. "Well, we found you outside the district of King William's Town. Obviously you were breaking your banning orders. So don't ask me stupid questions!"

Peter then asked on what charge he was being held.

Lieutenant Oosthuizen thought about this for a while. He turned to the black sergeant who was writing the report saying, "Just write down that he was carrying illegal pamphlets."

Steve and Peter were locked in one of the cells and neither spoke much during the long night. The security police were well-known for the cruel way in which they frequently treated political prisoners, and Steve and Peter had no idea what would happen to them.

Early the next morning their cell was unlocked. They were handcuffed and taken outside into the car park and forced into the back of a police car. Two security police officers got into the front and they drove at high speed towards Port Elizabeth.

In Port Elizabeth they were taken to the Sanlam Building, the headquarters of the security police in the Eastern Cape. They were taken up to the sixth floor and left in a little room with bars at the windows. They were each roughly handcuffed to the bars. Security police walked in and out of the room to laugh and pass rude comments at them while a photographer took shots of their faces.

Eventually a policeman called Major Fischer came into the room and showed Steve and Peter two warrants for their detention under Section 6 of the Terrorism Act. A group of policemen escorted them down to the ground floor of the building.

They were separated and each was surrounded by police officers. Then, with Peter in front and Steve a few paces behind, they were marched out to the car park. Peter was taken to a Kombi and was told to get in and lie face down on the floor between the seats.

As Steve passed, Peter looked up at him.

"Steve," he called out in a loud voice.

Steve stopped and called Peter's name too, and the two friends smiled in greeting. This was the last time Peter was to see his friend Steve Biko.

Peter was taken to Algoa Park police station where he was detained. He was left naked in his cell with one blanket and a mat. For several weeks Peter was beaten and questioned until he was moved to Kinkelbos police station on 31 October 1977. He was finally released from detention on 18 February 1979. He had spent a total of 533 days in prison.

Steve was taken to Walmer police station in Port Elizabeth. There he was questioned by the security police unit headed by Colonel Pieter Goosen. This man had a reputation for the cruel way in which he treated prisoners. In the hands of the police, Steve was so brutally treated that he never lived through it.

Four weeks later, on 14 September 1977, South Africans woke up to the shocking news:

> "Mr Biko, Honorary President of the Black People's Convention and the father of two children, is the 20th person to die in Security Force custody in 18 months."

> "Mr Steve Biko, the 30-year-old black leader, widely regarded as the founder of the Black Consciousness Movement in South Africa, died in detention on Monday (12 September)."

This report in *The Rand Daily Mail* went on to quote a statement by the Minister of Justice, Mr Jimmy Kruger. Kruger's statement suggested that Steve had been on a hunger strike for six days, and that he had become sick and died as a result.

The quote was taken from Minister Kruger's address to a Nationalist Party Congress. He opened his address with the following infamous comment:

> "I am not glad and I am not sorry about Mr Biko. It leaves me cold. I can say nothing to you. Any person who dies ... I shall also be sorry if I die."

The Minister of Justice had never before commented on the death of a detainee. In the light of the facts which would later be revealed, it became clear that Kruger was hiding the truth.

The "hunger strike" already sounded suspicious. Steve was strong and healthy and it was very unlikely that he would have died from not eating for six days. Also, the security police had given many suspicious reasons for detainees' deaths in the past. One detainee Solomon Modipane, for example, was said to have died after slipping on a piece of soap.

Many South Africans felt that the police were trying to avoid the blame for Steve's death. And the government did its best to ensure that the security police were not seen as responsible. Government-supporting newspapers such as *Die Burger* published articles which claimed that the police could not be held responsible for Steve's death.

Overseas countries also questioned the cause of Steve's death, and Minister Kruger was interviewed by a reporter from *The New York Times*. In the interview Minister Kruger said that a police assault was not the cause of Steve's death:

> "I personally do not believe this. I don't believe that my police have done anything wrong ... If there is anything wrong in the Biko case, I will be surprised ... There will be no cover up in the Biko case."

In reality, the cover up had already started, and Kruger himself was deeply involved in it.

7 People's Anger and Government Lies

There were still some charges against Steve at the time of his death. But he had never been found guilty of any crime while he lived. He had only been charged for breaking his banning orders, for example when he went into an educational building to write a law examination!

Steve was never arrested for encouraging violence nor accused of it. Only after his death did the police make their accusations. They said that they had documents which proved that Steve was a terrorist and that he had planned sabotage and riots.

There was a huge outcry from the black community and from all South Africans who fought apartheid. Large protest meetings were held in the main cities throughout the country. The people expressed their anger against Minister Kruger for saying that Steve had died from a hunger strike. And they blamed Kruger and his security police for Steve's death.

Donald Woods spoke at one of these protest meetings held at the University of Natal in Pietermaritzburg. This is part of his speech:

> "Steve Biko foresaw violence and bloodshed in South Africa. Don't we all? He could see it looming ahead. Don't we all? But to suggest that he encouraged it or desired it, is a terrible lie.
>
> "The main issue is that a key political figure in this country was detained in good health and within three weeks became the forty-fifth South African to die mysteriously in security police custody, and that it is

the duty of all free South Africans to question this mysterious death until those responsible have given adequate reply.

"I blame this government, in particular Prime Minister Vorster and Justice and Police Minister Kruger. They are the ones who have not only created the conditions causing violent unrest but they have ruled over a system of detention under which helpless people can be seized, tortured and assaulted without ever having had access to lawyers or friends or family – access not even denied to a criminal."

These protests continued and Minister Kruger made appearances on television. He talked about the dangers of Black Consciousness to whites and claimed that Steve had been involved in plotting violence.

The Afrikaner nationalist newspapers were filled with letters and articles of support for the government. *Die Burger* printed a front-page headline:

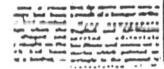

"Lyke en bloed gevra in Biko-pamflet"

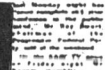

("Bodies and blood called for in Biko pamphlet")

As the heat of the protest rose, Minister Kruger backed down from saying that Steve had died from a hunger strike. Once again, he made a number of appearances on television. He again warned about the evils of Black Consciousness, and said that Steve had been fed intravenously when he became ill.

But during the post-mortem when Steve's body was examined to find out why he had died, the doctors found evidence of brain damage. Minister Kruger did not respond to these findings.

Steve's wife, Ntsiki, spoke about his death after the post-mortem had been completed:

"Steve Biko was a good man, he was a good father, but above all he was a leader. His death in detention did not come unexpected to me. I knew that because he was a man of such convictions and beliefs only death could stop him from what he believed in. But I am not satisfied with the way in which the government has said he died."

The first time Ntsiki heard of her husband's death was when she was notified by her sister and sister-in-law:

"No policemen informed me, nobody told me, and it was only through my sister-in-law and my sister that the news reached me. I was numb with shock. But I kept telling myself, and will continue to tell myself, that my husband died in a struggle, during a struggle for the liberation of the black man in South Africa."

Ntsiki also spoke about her two sons. Samora was two years old. Long after his father's death he would still run to the telephone whenever it rang and call Steve's name. Nkosinathi was six years old. He found it hard to accept the death of his father.

"I couldn't even bring myself to tell him that Steve was in detention again because he knew something was seriously wrong and said to me: 'No, Mama, you must not lie. I know he is dead.'"

The protests against Steve's death continued and calls were made for an inquest. An inquest is held when someone dies of unnatural causes, and when the government decides that there is no information that points to one specific person, or persons, to blame for the death. An investigation is then held to find out who is responsible for the death.

The government had started its white general election

campaign. Steve's family, friends and supporters were worried that the government would delay the inquest until after the election because it feared the bad publicity it was getting because of Steve's death while in their hands. They therefore increased their pressure for an inquest to be held as soon as possible.

The government responded in its usual way. It banned and detained a number of these people, including Percy Qoboza. He was taken away by the security police and his newspaper, *The World* was banned. David Russell of the Anglican Church and Donald Woods were banned and three BPC officials, namely Malusi Mpumlwana, Thenjiwe Mtintso and Kenny Rachidi, were detained. But the government did go ahead with the inquest before the general election.

There was strong evidence to suggest that the government was trying to cover up the truth in the Biko case. Because of this one may have expected a loss of support for the government. But instead, the election results showed increased support amongst the white electorate for the National Party.

8   The Funeral

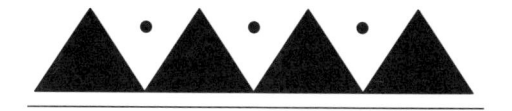

On 25 September 1977 thousands of people gathered in King William's Town. They had come to say *hamba kakuhle* ("goodbye") to one of their country's bravest sons.

But the police stopped thousands of mourners from attending Steve's funeral. Police also prevented bus convoys from leaving Johannesburg, Durban and Cape Town. Roadblocks were set up near King William's Town which turned hundreds of cars and many buses back. At the roadblocks were scores of determined police in camouflage uniforms armed with rifles and machine guns. Security policemen were also stationed on all the major roads into the town on 24 and 25 September. They stopped and searched all vehicles.

Dr Nthato Motlana, a speaker at the funeral, was stopped at one of the roadblocks in Johannesburg. He had to travel by aeroplane to attend the gathering. In his speech he said that he had watched as policemen hauled mourners off the buses in Soweto and assaulted them with batons.

The funeral ceremony lasted five hours. It was a protest rally against apartheid as well as a tribute to South Africa's greatly admired and brave young black leader.

The speakers were from organisations such as SASO and the BPC. The major theme of the speeches was the unity and strength of the black people. Its message was that the future South Africa would be one in which people would not be judged and separated according to colour.

There were also several hundred whites amongst the crowd. Personal friends of Steve, notably Reverend David Russell of the Anglican Church, Dr Francis Wilson, a lecturer at the

University of Cape Town, Donald and Wendy Woods, as well as members of the Progressive Federal Party (PFP), Helen Suzman, Zach de Beer and Alex Boraine. The PFP was the parliamentary party in opposition to the government at the time and its members were white liberals. Representatives from all the main overseas embassies and the Christian churches were also present.

The crowd of more than ten thousand people heard speaker after speaker warn the government that Steve Biko's death had pushed blacks further towards violence in their struggle for equal rights in South Africa. Reverend Desmond Tutu pleaded:

> "Please, please, for God's sake listen to us while there is still a possibility of reasonably peaceful change."

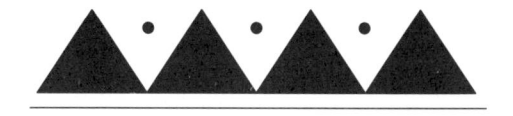

9 The Inquest

The Old Synagogue is in the centre of Pretoria. Inside the synagogue are "pews" for the "congregation" which seat about 200 people. The holy place had been transformed into raised seating for the judge, legal counsel, court stenographer, and witnesses.

For many years worshippers in the synagogue had heard the Lord's commandment that "Thou shall not kill". On Monday, 14 November 1977, however, people came to hear who had killed Steve Biko. The inquest had begun.

The Biko family (Steve's wife, mother, brother and sister) sat up front on a bench. The proceedings were in Afrikaans. Steve's family did not understand this language very well, so a young man sat with them acting as an interpreter.

The two front rows were reserved for the press. These rows were filled with reporters from all the main South African newspapers, as well as journalists from other countries in the world. The daily proceedings of the inquest were published every day in *The Rand Daily Mail*. Never before had there been so much publicity at an inquest of someone who had died in detention.

It is important to remember that an inquest is not a trial. There is no "accused" and no "defence". It is a public inquiry. A prosecutor presents all the evidence, a magistrate heads the inquiry, and two medical assessors help the magistrate to examine the medical evidence.

In the Biko inquest the security police and doctors were questioned in order to find out if they had fulfilled their duties in accordance with the law. Both the Biko family and the police and doctors had their own lawyers. These lawyers also had the right to question all the witnesses.

Outside the court, reporters hoisted television cameras onto their shoulders. Young police officers in blue uniforms walked about carrying guns and looking grim. German Shepherd dogs barked viciously from police vans. .

Every day during the inquest proceedings, hundreds of black people gathered on the pavements outside. The numbers would slowly increase, and as people came out of the synagogue they would start singing songs of freedom and defiance with their fists raised high in the air.

The security policemen who had been involved in the interrogation of Steve and who were responsible for his well-being, and the doctors who had been called in to examine his condition, were all called to the witness stand.

All the witnesses and almost all the court officials joined together to hide the cause of Steve's death, and to protect those who were responsible. The only person who could have given an accurate account of what had happened part of the way was Peter Jones. But he was in detention and was not allowed to appear as a witness.

The court heard that Steve had been kept naked in his cell for many days with his legs chained in leg irons. He had also been questioned for long periods by the security police. The police told of a scuffle between Steve and the five policemen and they said that Steve had hit the back of his head against the wall. They claimed that Steve had suffered his brain injuries from hitting his head against the wall.

Mr Sidney Kentridge appeared for the Biko family. He tried to show that there were clear flaws in this story. But the security police and the doctors stuck to their version of the story.

The magistrate announced that Steve had died from head injuries that had probably been caused during a scuffle, and that the police were not to blame.

The dismay and betrayal of hope showed on people's faces in the court-room. They, like millions of others throughout South Africa and abroad, were outraged at the outcome of the inquest.

The former President of the British Law Society, Sir David Napley, also attended the inquest. He had been invited by the Association of Law Societies in South Africa. Sir David was one of the most knowledgeable and experienced legal men in England. He felt strongly that the inquest was biased in favour of the police.

What follows is a summary of the story that came out during the inquest of Steve's death. The story shows clearly how the police and doctors hid the truth about the cause of Steve's death.

Steve Biko and Peter Jones were arrested on 18 August 1977. They were detained under Section 6 of the Terrorism Act. The two men were separated, and for the next 20 days Steve was kept at Walmer police station.

Steve was not allowed to wear any clothes and his legs were chained together with thick iron chains. He was not even allowed out of his cell for air or exercise. His daily ration of food was soup, *amarhewu* (a sour maize drink), bread, jam and coffee. Steve refused to eat the soup and *amarhewu*, and he ate very little bread.

On 1 September a magistrate visited Steve in his cell, and Steve complained that he had not even been allowed to wash himself. He asked the magistrate for water, soap, a washcloth and a comb so that he could wash himself.

"Is it compulsory that I have to be naked?" Steve asked the magistrate.

"I have been naked since I came here."

The magistrate did not reply.

On 6 September the security police took Steve from Walmer police station to Room 619 of the Sanlam Building in Port Elizabeth. Here he was interrogated by five security men. The police said that they had been with Steve from 10:30 in the morning until 18:00 in the evening. From 18:00 onwards, until the following morning, he was left in the care of the night squad, naked and handcuffed, with one leg chained to a grille.

The head of the interrogation team, Major Harold Snyman, arrived at 7:00 the following morning. He said that he had removed Steve's leg-irons and handcuffs and that Steve had attacked the security men. They said that it was during this fight that Steve had received the blows that caused brain damage and resulted in his death five days later. The police were unable to continue their interrogation because of Steve's condition.

Colonel Goosen was informed about this "incident", and at 7:30 in the morning he arrived at Room 619. He said that Steve's speech was unclear and that he had talked in a slurred manner. There was also a visible swelling on his upper lip.

The District Surgeon, Dr Ivor Lang, was called in and he examined Steve. Colonel Goosen asked Dr Lang to write out a medical certificate stating that there was no abnormality in Steve's condition. Dr Lang complied with Colonel Goosen's request.

That evening the security police tried to interrogate Steve again but he was totally unresponsive. He was left lying on a mat on the floor of the office for the rest of the day and night. He was still handcuffed and chained in leg-irons.

By the following day Steve had still not eaten and Colonel

Goosen called Dr Lang again. Dr Lang noticed no change in his condition, and asked if Dr Benjamin Tucker, the Chief District Surgeon, would examine Steve with him. The two doctors decided to move him to the prison hospital.

A specialist doctor was consulted and he checked Steve for brain damage. The doctors decided that there wasn't any brain damage. They said that Steve should just be kept under observation.

On the morning of 11 September the security police took Steve from his hospital bed back to a cell at Walmer police station. He was left naked under some blankets on a mat on the cement floor of the cell.

A few hours later a warder found Steve lying on the floor, glassy-eyed with foam at his mouth. Colonel Goosen was told of Steve's condition, and he called Dr Tucker who examined Steve once again.

Colonel Goosen decided to send Steve to the prison hospital in Pretoria and Dr Tucker felt that Steve would manage the journey of 1 628 km by road. He was left naked and handcuffed on the floor of the back of a Land-Rover with nothing except a flask of water.

Steve arrived at the Pretoria prison on 11 September, 11 hours after leaving Port Elizabeth. He was carried into the prison hospital and left on the floor of a cell. Several hours later, on 12 September, a newly-qualified doctor, with no medical information about Steve other than that he was refusing to eat, ordered an intravenous drip.

Steve died later that night.

Conclusion

What did Steve Biko do to die such a cruel death at the hands of the security police? They claimed that he was a dangerous man yet they did not even take him to court to try to prove this.

Steve was seen as a threat because he stood up against the apartheid government with the Black Consciousness Movement. Since the early 1970s Steve and his followers had worked hard to unite black people against apartheid, and the government in turn used the strength of its laws and its powerful security police to destroy him.

Steve was the 45th person to die in police custody since 1963, when detention without trial was first introduced in South Africa. Eight years after Steve's death two of the doctors who had treated him, Dr Benjamin Tucker and Dr Ivor Lang, were found guilty of unprofessional conduct by the disciplinary committee of the South African Medical and Dental Council. The council finally certified that the doctors had not fulfilled their duty to give Steve the correct and full medical care that he needed.

Steve has been called the father of Black Consciousness in South Africa. He was also the person who saw Black Consciousness as the path to a non-racial, democratic South Africa. He left black people with the important belief that they should feel pride in themselves and not feel inferior.

He stood for a new confidence among blacks and for a policy which said:

> "We don't only want to get rid of apartheid; we also want to get rid of the total exploitation in this country of black people, which is not merely racial, not merely legislative, but also psychological, social and economic."

Steve looked forward to a non-racial, just and equal society in which a person's colour, religion and race would make no difference to his or her chances in life.

And so ends the sad but triumphant story of the young Steve of Ginsberg township who grew up to become one of South Africa's heroes. He was only 30 years old when he died but the name Bantu Stephen Biko has remained alive in South Africa over the years along with the other great leaders who have fought apartheid. His spirit is kept alive by the memory of his death in detention but, much more importantly, by the seeds of pride and justice which he sowed in South African soil.

A portrait of Steve Biko by Daily Dispatch *artist Don Kenyon*

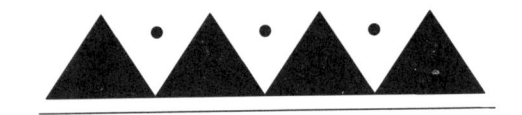

Learn these Words and Phrases

amenities: facilities available to the public, usually for leisure or entertainment, such as parks, sports fields, cinemas, restaurants. (see page 13)

banned: when a person is legally prevented from living a normal life in society by restrictions of movement, speech and association that are placed on him/her for a specified period of time. (see page 19)

discriminated: treated unfairly. (see page 12)

dominated: took the lead/had the upper hand. (see page 5)

electorate: all the people who make up the voters in a country. (see page 38)

exploitation: to deny people their basic rights as fellow human beings. (see page 47)

expressed: put one's thoughts into words. (see page 8)

grievances: problems and complaints. (see page 8)

gumba music: a special kind of African music based more on interesting harmony than on melody. (see page 21)

infamous: having a bad reputation. (see page 33)

intravenous drip: when glucose and minerals are passed into a patient's body through his/her veins with the use of a drip. This helps prevent the patient from getting weak or dying. (see page 45)

liberation: to free or release. (see page 37)

oppressed: denied basic human rights. (see page 15)

paternalistic: when a person shows concern for others but thinks that he/she knows what is best for them. (see page 17)

reinforce: to strengthen with additional effort. (see page 16)

scholarship: money given to an excellent student to further his/her studies. (see page 4)

self-sufficient: not dependent on others. (see page 16)

silhouetted: outlined or thrown into shadow by a light background. (see page 1)

solitary confinement: when a prisoner is kept alone in his/her cell and has no contact with anyone during this time. (see page 22)

stenographer: the person who types up the court proceedings. (see page 41)

study by correspondence: students who cannot study full-time at university can register for degrees with UNISA and study from home. The university sends students assignments by post and once the work has been completed it is sent back to be marked. (see page 19)

synagogue: a building used for worship in the Jewish religion. (see page 41)

underground movement: a movement or organisation which is forced to operate in secret because of laws prohibiting its existence. (see page 28)

veld: countryside. (see page 1)

witness: a person who has been involved in, or has any knowledge about the case, is called to the stand to answer questions and tell the court what he/she knows. (see page 24)

Activities

1

What have you learned about Steve Biko and the important role he played in South African history?

Choose the correct answer and write it down in your exercise book:

(a) Steve Biko and other black students decided to break away from NUSAS and form SASO because
 (i) NUSAS was not a multiracial organisation
 (ii) White students in NUSAS could not identify with the problems the black students faced
 (iii) all the NUSAS members were imprisoned by the government

(b) When students from SASO went into Newfarm to build new homes and the community just looked on, they realised that
 (i) the people were ungrateful and did not appreciate help
 (ii) the people did not want anybody to help them
 (iii) they should have discussed the matter with them first to avoid misunderstanding

(c) The Black Consciousness Movement believed that it was important to call black people "black" because
 (i) it was a fashionable term used in America
 (ii) it was a positive term to use instead of "non-white", which was a negative term used by the government
 (iii) it was easy to pronounce

(d) The concept "self-help" was very important in the Black Consciousness Movement because it was felt that
   (i) black people had to rely on themselves and not the government for help
   (ii) it was no use relying on other people
   (iii) it was the cheapest way to get things done

(e) The government tried to stop Steve Biko from working in the Black Consciousness Movement by
   (i) banning the Black Consciousness Movement
   (ii) banning him, which meant that he could not participate in any political work
   (iii) imprisoning him on Robben Island

(f) The uprising of 1976 was very important in the history of black opposition to apartheid because
   (i) it was a rebirth of widespread opposition to apartheid and served as a bridge connecting the younger and older generation of black South Africans
   (ii) black children weren't forced to attend government schools anymore
   (iii) the government decided to negotiate with black leaders for the first time

(g) Steve Biko's death in police detention was explained to the public by the Minister of Justice although this had never happened with any other detainee in the past. The reason for this was that
   (i) the government realised that they were wrong and wanted to apologise
   (ii) the government introduced a new policy regarding detainees
   (iii) the government realised that Steve Biko was an important black leader and that his death could not be ignored in the same way other detainees' deaths had been ignored

(h) At Steve Biko's funeral the crowd of more than ten thousand people were comforted by the message that

   (i) strengthened by black unity, they could look forward to a future South Africa where people would not be judged and separated by colour

   (ii) Steve Biko was a good man

   (iii) Steve Biko's death had forced the government to admit that apartheid was wrong, and they were now willing to work towards a just society

(i) Sir David Napley's presence at the inquest proceedings was important because

   (i) he could teach South African Law Societies how to conduct proper inquests

   (ii) he was able to force the authorities to hold a fair and just inquest

   (iii) he was an experienced and respected British lawyer and he felt that the inquest was in favour of the police

(j) The government would not allow Peter Jones out of detention to give evidence at the inquest because

   (i) he was too ill at the time

   (ii) he and Steve Biko were arrested together and Peter could give an accurate account of the circumstances under which they were being held by the police

   (iii) they wished to protect him from possible danger from his enemies outside of prison

2

Match the words in the left column with a description from the right column. Write the correct form down in your exercise book and add a sentence of your own to each one to explain it more fully.

(a)	Apartheid	is a town where many of Johannesburg's black workers live (and where students started protesting against black education in 1976).
(b)	Soweto	is a town where 69 black demonstrators were shot by the police in 1960.
(c)	Jimmy Kruger	is a black leader imprisoned on Robben Island at the time of Biko's death.
(d)	Steve Biko	is a movement which aimed to unite and strengthen black people (and to overcome feelings of black inferiority).
(e)	Black Consciousness	is a system of laws that separate black people from white people.
(f)	Nelson Mandela	is the man who said: "I am not sorry about Mr Biko. It leaves me cold."
(g)	Donald Woods	is regarded as the father of the Black Consciousness Movement in South Africa.
(h)	Sharpeville	was a close friend of Steve Biko and editor of the *Daily Dispatch*.

3

Look at the table below in which some of the events in the life of Steve Biko are outlined. In places certain information has been left out. Try to supply the missing information, writing it down in your exercise book.

_____, King William's Town	Bantu Stephen Biko born.
1963, _____	Sparked off Steve's interest in politics.
1965	Steve won a scholarship to study at _____.
December 1968	_____, a black student organisation was formed.
1970	Marriage to _____. They had _____ children.
_____	Steve expelled from university.
1973	Steve _____ by the government. He was forced to go from Durban to _____ and stay there for _____ years.
May 1976	Steve was called as _____ in the trial of nine students. Here Steve could explain the philosophy of _____.
_____	Soweto, police opened fire, killing or injuring students.
18 August 1977	Steve Biko and Peter Jones were _____ near Grahamstown.
12 September 1977	_____ in police custody.

4

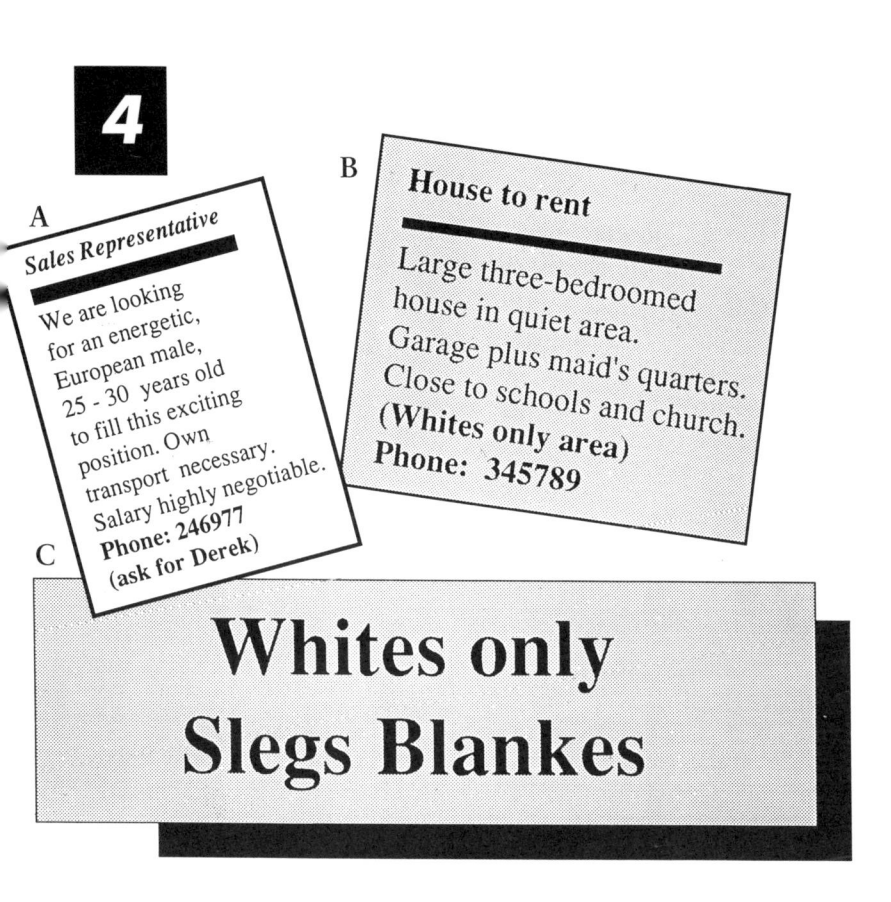

A
Sales Representative

We are looking for an energetic, European male, 25 - 30 years old to fill this exciting position. Own transport necessary. Salary highly negotiable.
Phone: 246977
(ask for Derek)

B
House to rent

Large three-bedroomed house in quiet area. Garage plus maid's quarters. Close to schools and church. **(Whites only area)**
Phone: 345789

C

Whites only
Slegs Blankes

Advertisements A and B are similar to those that could have appeared in newspapers in Biko's lifetime. The sign marked C was a familiar sight on beaches, park benches, post offices, bus stops etc.

(a) Name the apartheid law which applied to each of the above notices.
(b) Who is being discriminated against in each notice? Explain how.
(c) Do you still see examples of advertisements and signs like this? If so, where?
(d) Speak to a relative or friend (mother, father, aunt, grandfather etc.) and find out how they experienced these laws. Does it differ from your experiences today? Explain.

5

The Black Consciousness Movement started up community projects with the emphasis on self-help.

(a) If you had had the opportunity to work with Steve Biko and his friends, how would you have contributed towards these self-help schemes?
(b) Are there any self-help schemes in your area where you could make a contribution? If so, how?

6

Dramatisation

Write and act out a script which depicts a meeting of the Black People's Convention (BPC). Your characters should include Steve Biko and other leaders as well as ordinary members of the BPC. Your script should include different opinions and attitudes expressed at the meeting.

7

Essay Question

Describe the contribution that Steve Biko made to the fight against apartheid in South Africa.

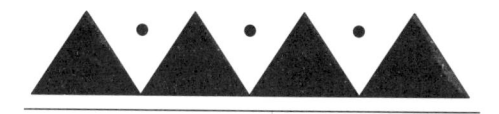

More Books about Biko

Would you like to read more about Steve Biko and Black Consciousness? Here are a few more titles which you may enjoy.

No. 46 – Steve Biko by Hilda Bernstein.

Hilda Bernstein is a South African writer who has played an active role in the liberation movement. Here she writes a documentary account of Steve Biko's death and the inquest which followed. The book was published by the International Defence Aid Fund in London in 1978.

I Write What I Like: a selection of his writings by Steve Biko. Ed. A. Stubbs

Father Aelred Stubbs was a personal friend of Steve Biko, and has also been very committed to the fight against apartheid. He compiled this collection of Steve's writings as a tribute to Steve's thoughts and ideas. The book covers the basic philosophy of Black Consciousness, African culture, and Western involvement in apartheid. It was published by Heinemann in Oxford in 1978.

South Africa: A Different Kind of War by Julie Frederikse.

This is an interesting compilation of both factual and personal anecdotes of South African life under apartheid. It contains photographs, copies of pamphlets and interviews with South Africans from all walks of life. It was published by Ravan in Johannesburg in 1986.

The Unbreakable Thread by Julie Frederikse

Julie Frederikse provides a historical overview of the origin, development and strength of non-racialism in South Africa. The book also contains interviews with prominent veteran activists and the new generation of leaders. It was published by Ravan in Johannesburg in 1990.

The Fruit of Fear: June 16 by Peter Magubane

This is a vivid recollection of 16 June 1976 and focuses on the horror and cruelty of police oppression. It primarily contains photographs taken during the riots. The book was published by Skotaville in Johannesburg in 1986.

Foundations of the New South Africa by John Pampallis

John Pampallis is a South African writer who has played an active role in the liberation movement. In this book he focuses on the role of all South Africans in the making of the country's history. He provides an overview of the liberation and labour movements and includes extracts from important documents and interviews. It was published by Maskew Miller Longman in Cape Town in 1991.

The Testimony of Steve Biko by Steve Biko. Ed. M. Arnold

This book contains a brief look at Steve Biko's life and contains his full testimony during the trial of the students in 1976. His strength and brilliance as a political thinker and advocate of Black Consciousness is clearly conveyed. The book was published by Panther in England in 1979.

Biko by Donald Woods

Donald Woods was a close friend of Steve Biko. In this book Donald talks about their friendship and how it enlarged his own political awareness. He provides a more personal account of Steve Biko's political activities and also focuses on his death and the inquest which followed. The book was published by Penguin in London in 1987.